The Field

The Field

Poems by Rhina P. Espaillat

David Robert Books

Published by David Robert Books
P.O. Box 541106
Cincinnati, OH 45254-1106

ISBN: 978-1-62549-315-6

Poetry Editor: Kevin Walzer
Business Editor: Lori Jareo

Visit us on the web at www.davidrobertbooks.com

Acknowledgments/ Thanks/ Dedication

I am grateful, as always, to the Powow River Poets, for their loving companionship and honest judgment.

My profound thanks to the editors and staff of the following publications and websites, where several of the poems in this collection have appeared:

Agenda; Alabama Literary Review; American Arts Quarterly; Angle Journal; Caprice; Connecticut River Review; The Dark Horse; The Emily Dickinson Award Anthology; The Evansville Review; A Formal Feeling Comes: Poems in Form by Contemporary Women; The Hudson Review; Iambs and Trochees; The Jewish Women's Literary Annual; Landscapes with Women: Four American Poets; Light Quarterly; The Lyric; Margie; Measure; Medicinal Purposes; Mid-American Poetry Review; Mobius; The National Poetry Review; Oberon; Off the Coast; The Piedmont Literary Review; Post Road; The Raintown Review; Rattle; Ship of Fools; SpinDrifter; Stone Canoe; The Texas Poetry Review; Think; Bottegheoscure.net; Light Online; Lucidrhythms.com; PerContra.net; Mezzocammin.com; The Newington Cropsey website.

Dedication

For Philip and Lauren, Warren and Lori, and Bill and Colleen,
whose unfailing love keeps me whole.

Table of Contents

Just Stopping

Naked

Idle Comments

Bistro

Watching young lovers do what lovers do
with eyes shut tightly, you forget the rest,
how time unsays the words, however true.
Watching young lovers do what lovers do
you almost warn them, Stop! As if you knew
some better thing than this by which they're blessed.
Watching young lovers do what lovers do,
with eyes shut tightly you forget the rest.

Crossword on the Bus

"Why did you call me 'Charlie'? Yeah, you did.
Go get your mother on the phone. Out? Where?
So who's with you? OK, put Grandma on.
Yeah, fine, I'm good. So, say, why did my kid
just call me 'Charlie'? Is your daughter there?
You jerking me around? What gone? Where gone?
That's not my business? Listen, I don't care...
Hello, hello! Pick up, you bitch!"

                                   I'm drawn
to look up from my puzzle—if I can
without his noticing—but do not dare.
Silence like knives, now that he's snapped the lid
of his cell phone. Who knows when words began
hardening into silence for this man?
I hunt for words to pencil on the grid.

Hotel

Noises behind the wall kept him awake
till late: a bickering that seemed so near—
as if inside the bedding—he could make
sense, almost, of words he strained to hear
despite himself. After a shallow dream
he woke to morning bleeding through the gap
where the drapes failed to meet. A rush of steam
urged him to up and out, and then a tap
turned by some stranger in the neighboring shower.
He knew he couldn't face the rain that slid
down fourteen stories of a grimy tower
to midtown traffic. But he rose, and did,
and at the corner diner stirred the cup
stirred by the silent stranger looking up.

Idle Comments

After the service, when the neighbors left,
breathing their last condolences like prayers,
it startled him that he was not bereft.

He'd enjoyed lunch, in fact. The last eclairs
still on their sugared doily, rolls of ham,
his wife's old cousin's gift of home-made jam,
all hinted at the care others would take,
henceforth, of him and of his few affairs.
Someone would look through papers, and the heirs
would be informed; there would be claims to make
and forms to file; his son would sell the car.

He smiled and turned to tell her so, before
remembering that she was much too far
to hear his idle comments any more.

Matinee

A stranger in a splint, shoulder to thumb,
is clearly relishing the show: in fact,
laughing out loud beside me, overcome
by Aristophanes. But he is wracked
when, half oblivious of his bones (because
pleasure distracts us from the carnal place
that pain assigns us), he attempts applause.
Each time he does it, scribbled on his face
the body's memo reads, *I told you so*.
You'd think he would remember, but I see
him lift both hands, as if he didn't know
that he will flinch again, when memory
repeats the lesson he must learn anew.
My palms are raw with making noise for two.

Rite

The summer drownings have begun:
the seventh—and it's only May!—
has brought this ordinary day
a new capacity to stun.

They seem familiar on the screen:
the would-be rescuer whose dive
failed, and the family of five
just four, now that the prankster teen,

who loved to tease the tide, is caught
in strands of silky blue, and bound,
for once, to matter more profound.
Now from the depth of their one thought,

scanning the river's purling foam,
they bow, like suppliants in a frieze,
as if still hoping to appease
currents that might return him home.

A Rondeau for Rachel

In Rachel's room the books are stacked
at random on tall shelves, and packed
three layers deep, with items piled
criss-cross on what's beneath—a wild
Tower of Babel all knick-knacked:

Here, Chinese puzzles; there, a cracked
jewel-case that begs to be ransacked;
and who's this sunny, curly child
            in Rachel's room?

Rachel herself, crookedly tacked
beside one shelf, caught in the act:
smiling, as years ago she smiled,
and now for me, the guest beguiled
by girl and print and artifact
            in Rachel's room.

We Regret to Inform You

How can she save her son, still in his teens—
still living, while the silence is unbroken—
from what this officer in his dress greens
must do with words that threaten to be spoken?

The bomb or bullet, ceremonial knife
or flame (she will not hear which one it was)
struggle to find a foothold, spring to life
on her New Hampshire porch, right now, to cause—

but no, no one must name it, at her door
where he says "Ma'am," insistent, through a crack
he cannot pry a millimeter more,
she cannot close again to turn him back.

One Defense

After the Rally

A clown with an odd hairdo and a list
of *parasites* (some tilling the same ground
where they were born) he vows to see dismissed,
walled out for good, or worse; a bark-like sound
some of us heard before, scornful and brash;
an audience with the rapt look of recruits.
No weapons, though; no patch of black mustache;
no lightning banners or stiff-armed salutes.
This replay may be nothing more than funny;
maybe he hasn't bought the power he needs—
not yet—despite his dragon-hoard of money;
maybe this blessed soil resists the seeds
that grew and spread from both banks of the Rhine.
Maybe this isn't nineteen-thirty-nine.

A Ghost-Written Post-Suicide Note

for Kalief Browder, 22, i. m.

Man Held at Rikers for 3 Years Without Trial Hangs Himself.
New York *Times*, Obituary, Tuesday, June 9, 2015

First, what I knew. To Whom It May Concern:

The guards were paid to beat me in my cell.
Confinement would, in Solitary, turn
to howling from an unseen crowd in hell.
Behind the screen's unwavering, sullen stare
they monitored my thoughts, reading them all.
They followed me, and bruised me everywhere.
The noose around my neck broke my last fall.

And now, the things I never came to know:

Who took away my freedom and my youth?
The years stolen from me—where did they go?
How do my judges sleep? Who hid the truth,
or stole the knapsack someone said I stole?
To whom or what should I commend my soul?

One Defense

One man regards another as a brute,
like those his kinfolks purchased for their own
use, like cattle, invisible and mute.
But sometimes, unexpectedly alone
in the soul's light—dim, but not wholly out—
the once-possessed confront him, and he sees
a horrifying likeness: there's no doubt
this is a man. Even on his knees,
or shackled, or in flames, or dangling noosed,
clearly a man, like him. What strange distress:
the would-be repossessor is reduced
by silent accusations. How confess
the common human blood shared with this man?
He needs to shed that blood. And knows he can.

Rhymes with *Banish*

First she chimes "Nine-one-one." In broken English
he stammers for "help, please," and someone Spanish-
speaking to talk to. But before he's finished,
she says, "We all speak English, sir, not Spanish."
After a pause he says, sounding astonished,
"In Lawrence—I live here—nobody Spanish?"
as if to ask her, "When did we all vanish?"
But she is firm and curt: "We all speak English—
just English—here; we don't know any Spanish."
As she says it on tape it sounds like "punish."

[On August 3, 2015, in Lawrence, MA (an immigrant city where a high
proportion of the population comes from Latin America and Asia), a 911
responder received a call from a man in need of help who asked for a Spanish-
speaking person to whom he could describe his emergency.

When challenged after the incident over her inadequate response to the caller,
the responder explained that she didn't turn him over to one of the Spanish-
speaking workers available because she could tell from the caller's tone of voice
that there was nothing seriously wrong.]

Significant Other

This is for you, Miss Ridley, who made clear
in 'forty-seven—high school, junior year—
that you would not pronounce, much less condone,
barbaric names like ours. You made it known
at once that we would change, like obscure books
translated. And our disbelieving looks
at roll call never altered your idea
that I'd learn to be "RYE nah," as Sophia
Papadopoulos must answer to "Soh FIE ah"
and shy Maria Guzman became "Maw RYE ah."

You could not whittle us into those new
fictions remade in your own image, true
daughters of Albion; we were marked by then
by sound and sign, the legacies of men
and women of all stripes, from every shore.
We recognized ourselves, the names we bore,
solid as coins history had imprinted,
unwilling to be melted and reminted.
But every morning, doggedly set right,
you would repeat the wrong. You were not bright.

How did it end? Not badly: six refused,
at last, to answer "Present." You accused
us of impertinence, and sent us to
the Principal herself. We never knew
her verdict; we were quietly dismissed
after an uneventful hearing, and the list
bearing our names and her few notes remained
on her oak desk. Our records went unstained.

And by the next day's roll call we discerned
change in your method, and our names returned,
pronounced not well, but, well, the best you could.

We learned a lot from you: to define "good"
in broader terms than yours; how to defend
ourselves within what law we would amend;
how to make room, among us all, for each;
how not to be afraid; how not to teach!
How some, recalled for scenes we do not miss,
give us our arms. Too late, I give you this.

Two Cameos

I: Rita

Daughter of Spanish dancers who would train
her in their art, back when her name was still
Cansino, she was beautiful—but then,
who wasn't, in the movies? *Entertain,*
that was the mission: and to fill the bill
you needed looks to please the businessmen
who made the films. And talent—but again,
beauty came first, and glamor that could thrill
the glamor-starved at once, with the first scene.
Her name, though: would it play in Centerville?
Wouldn't the sticks, they thought, prefer some plain
English whispering *money,* for a queen?
OK, she would be *Hayworth* for the screen:
now that says *regal.* Not a word of Spain.

II: Hattie

As in *McDaniel*—talent robed in fat,
the first Black winner of an Oscar—played
Mammy, who hovered over Vivian Leigh.
Some resented her role, her *dis* and *dat,*
the humbling of her gifts; they felt betrayed
by her portrayal of their race. But she,
who laughed at symbols, said *I'd rather be
acting the part on screen and being paid
seven hundred a day*—a royal sum—
than earning seven as a real live maid.
After she spoke on Oscar night, they sat

her in the back, where she'd been summoned from,
the Negro Section. Look how far we've come.
Who paid to get us here, and paid with what?

Two Tenements

Built side by side, two tenements, so near—
three or four feet between them, if that much—
that if a hand from one were to appear
and open any window, it could touch
a neighbor's hand where I would have it come
out of the facing window. Picture them,
leaving behind the gloom they venture from
to bridge the gap, a braided double stem
sprouting out of each winter to say *spring*.
But, no, the panes are blackened on each side
and every window shut, and not a thing
tendrils across and over that divide
to brighten the stark bricks, the dark below.
And still the passing eye would have it so.

...That Doesn't...

True, but there is the self-sequestering
something
at work in the protector of what's his.
There is
the magnet's other pole—there always was—
that does
not want the walls to tumble down, because,
how can one be secure without the wall
and the impulse to *mend it?* After all,
something there is that *does.*

A Spanish Galleon Contemplates the Future

Above me, sky; and down below, the stream.
Loud on the wind that fills my swelling sails,
A swarm of raucous seabirds dive and scream,
circling the rigging and the churning wake,
where they hunt their food and ride the gales.
Do they speak, in the exultant noise they make,
for the future, unknown and not yet real,
but working to become?

                      Under me,
the current drags its weight against my keel,
like chains pulling me home to Spain again.
Wind and water keep me bound in two
directions: toward treasures of the sea,
and the familiar soil that bred these men,
my rough, ambitious, restless, ruthless crew!

They also hunt—money, adventure, land—
and carry with them everything they've known:
that heavy burden, poverty; the cross;
the force of power in another's hand;
reckless energy; the need to act alone;
a taste for profit from another's loss.

How will they see the stranger—a new race—
another's food and customs, gods and speech,
weapons and rituals, color, odor, face?
How will that other see them? As if each
were his own man, or as a faceless horde
to be received with loathing and reviled?

How will the future judge and then record
Spain's juncture with the *undiscovered wild*?

España: the word ripples with pride
in its long history of art, design,
books in which the words are jewels arrayed
as in a royal crown, or as each line
of my body—calligraphy in oak—
flows like a living being on the tide.

Blessed by the Virgin's eyes, my gallery
wears railings whose medallioned squares evoke
balconies, and the gallant artistry
with which the lines of Spanish verse are made.

Maybe these sailors, as live transplants do,
will take root where they anchor, and at last
earn what they seek to conquer: not through war,
but through labor, the dream of something new,
generous, risky, never seen before,
more just and free than the retreating past.

The Field

Aftermath

Poor mush I swatted with an angry hand
simply for being, and for being still,
forgive me, though you cannot understand
how blows, not always meant, land where they land,
whatever else it is one needs to kill.

April Foolery

Winter laid down the law: *Keep the shades drawn;*
go decent to your grave;
even in thought, be decorous; behave;
keep your old habits on.

But look, new shoots are sneaking through the duff,
fresh lichen paints the bark,
and fields strip off their last snow, as if stark
naked were good enough.

The sky has shed its rain, and shallow pools
are wearing only sky,
as if inciting all the world to sly
infractions of the rules!

Icicles

I had been thinking—as we like to do,
we idle versifiers who contrive
yokes of resemblance to make one from two—
I had been thinking how cold winds, which drive
light things, may lend to weight a shapeliness
that makes it firm and mimics constancy.

Those crystal tears, for instance, should grow less
as drop by drop they drip, but each degree
lost with the setting sun prolongs them so
that each becomes a stream—a cataract—
of mourning, hard with habit, until no
consolation seems enough, and tact
must look away and honor such despair.

But no, one gust, capricious, with a sound
like passing laughter, tugs once more, and there:
my whole conceit in fragments on the ground.
So much for metaphor, that with its sly
embroidery seduces us to tales,
reduces us to liars by and by.
And maybe just as well, the way it fails.

The Jury

In a bare tree,
four strangers gathered from afar
slipped into talk, as travelers do.
First Eagle said, "How strange they are,

these creatures lately come to climb
our cliffs and spy upon our brood.
They have no constancy, but drift
from mood to mood:

first, wanton slaughter, and now zeal
to build our hunted tribe again.
I cannot fathom them at all."
"They are called Men,"

said Pigeon, "and I know them well.
I've learned their secret. All they use,
from day to day, to guide their steps,
is just their shoes.

It's true, my friends. In new spiked boots
yesterday's farmer struts the street,
turned killer, and tomorrow dies
derelict, with rag-bound feet.

More out of sympathy than need,
I gather their spilled crumbs to know
toward what new grief
their wayward shoes would have them go."

"And yet," said Sparrow, "I have known
some who would leave their lighted nest
to scatter seed, through razor winds,
for our sake, lest

we hunger through December days.
I've seen them fling their gaze above
their comforts, to pursue us with
something like love."

"True," Vulture said, "for they love me
and have my welfare much in mind.
In Leningrad, in Lebanon
men were most kind

and nourished me with their own young.
Vietnam, Verdun, Angola, Troy,
Thermopylae...the love of men
is my chief joy."

"Well, that's as may be," Eagle said,
"but they are feeble things at best.
Condemned to winglessness, they creep
in their own shadow, flight-obsessed,

a sad smudge upon the earth,
half-willingly erased at last.
We will possess our own again,
when they have passed."

Lesson

Wind, let me teach you
to make a winter evening.
First, wash the sky;

suspend it above
my neighbor's roof; secure it
with early stars.

Stitch carefully from
maple to maple a thin
humming wire

clotted with sparrows;
spangle the earth with silver
tatters of rain.

Clear a blue circle
above the shivering of
wild cherry trees

rubbing their fingers;
gather the last light there, and
hang up the moon.

Lettuce

Held under water to remove the sand
and, sometimes, tiny slugs, or specks with wings,
it will unfold, bend backward like a hand
protesting innocence. The center springs
apart to show the core, a knot of pale
blossom the naked color of March snow.
Turned upside down, it dons the coat of mail
of its tough leather green, as if to go
into some animal disguise of hide.
Lactuca sativa, the family
Compositae, so says the garden guide:
kin to the daisy, then. But what I see
suggests a closer kinship with the rose,
whose open heart remembers how to close.

Midwinter View

How changeless at first glance, these days that glide,
docile beads on a string, till side by side,
in retrospect, they coax the eye to see
distinctions where it saw identity:
this bead duller than that, and that less round,
one dimpled. Or suppose a figured ground
where pale denial whispers into view,
once bolder patterns tell what they hold true.
Such images instruct, as if one were
no mere collector, but a connoisseur
of sameness, an authority on gray,
interpreter of silences that say
what must divide one moment from the next,
with just minute mutations of the text.

Parsnip

Cut it across, a bit below the crown,
immerse it in a tablespoon or so
of water in a shallow dish, tamp down
with cotton, keep it moist, and it will grow.

Though why it grows, or why it sends a shoot
feathering toward the light of the first day—
without a single filament of root
to feed or anchor it—I cannot say.

How can it thrive more than a week or ten
days on the sill, nourished by nothing more
than a green urgency to live again?
And yet it sprouts as if it meant to soar,
this minute palm, commanded by some word
no less compelling than it is absurd.

Peacock

At the small local farm where toddlers walk
bravely with geese but circumspect with sheep,
behind a fence that neither wants to leap,
a ghostly clamor, an unearthly squawk
rings like a summons from some royal keep.

And there, far more than kingly, self-absorbed
as any god, and gorgeous as the night,
this barnyard apparition spreads his orbed
and iridescent plumes not meant for flight,
but for display and sacrificial rite.

What can these children make, with their two eyes
apiece, of countless staring pupils pinned,
unblinking, to his heavenly disguise,
which shudders when he struts through dung that lies
amid shed feathers puffed by a rank wind?

Eden the morning after comes to mind:
the maker strolls alone among the trees
heavy with unplucked fruit, all left behind
by his lost creatures in the void he sees,
in whose unpeopled light he is confined.

But here the metaphor, of course, breaks down—
as metaphors should know enough to do—
leaving the children safe in our small town,
under diaphanous September blue
innocent now of all it ever knew.

Privacy

This is my post—my window on the day—
and not one sparrow foraging the last
cold berries, not one flake will tumble past
untallied, though the wind whisk it away.

A dozen shades of white and half a score
of grays make up the palette of this view—
or nearly, if I total in those few
discarded browns the maples lately wore.

And yet the scene remains (despite the eyes
intent on grasping all of it) unread:
Is something here not written down, but said?
Listening now, I strain to recognize

the speech, if not the script. But not the least
syllable I make out is meant for me:
I must be meant—if not content—to be
the unregarded stranger at the feast.

Whatever here wants to be understood—
if something does—doesn't have me in mind,
however much our paths are intertwined.
Some days I'm half inclined to say that's good.

Summer Work

*"I was away in Vermont busy with the business of
counting clouds."* —Tom Ryan, <u>The Undertoad</u>

Counting them, yes: and then
discovering again
how one and one make ten;

how what they try to be—
or are, or presently

become—shifts as they travel,
colliding to unravel,

fusing to come undone,
foaming around the sun,

spinning a web of goats,
stirring a dish of boats,

doodling a shark, dispersing
while I sit here a-versing.

Sometimes I think to try
some other work. But why?

And if I did, then who
would count the clouds? Would you?
And would the count be true?

The Field

The wind stopped breathing on the field.
At once the grass and its immense
meaningless turbulence
stood still, as in an instant sealed—
sun, stones and all—in sudden permanence.

Sobered then, done with all the churning
that lifts and multiplies the light,
each stalk halted, upright,
darkly attentive, as if learning
what voice had summoned it to be contrite.

But then I heard the wind relent:
it breathed, and blew the grasses free
of what had sobered me—
not them, since what a stillness "meant"
means nothing that a field of grass can see.

If only what's obliquely thought—
our brushes with the eerie—ended
like this, clearly intended
to spice the ordinary, not
to evoke darkness dimly comprehended.

Three Tenses of Light

for Andrew Anderson-Bell

Sky, meadow and marsh:
a trinity of waters,
three tenses of light.

Tattered horizon,
the far fringes of morning
where new light rises:

Daylight advancing,
igniting sudden loosestrife,
taking the meadow.

Cloud blue flecked with sun:
noon wavering, gold water
fringed with black grasses.

Nothing here to cast
shade, measure the afternoon's
retreat, its fading

fall into darkness
over marsh and meadow. Sky,
you patient watcher

of all creation,
bend to the sleeping water,
embrace it wholly

through the dark hours,

then rise to bring us, again,
light's benediction.

Two Crows

Two crows are pecking at the ice above
the skylight, with such loud, percussive speed
they've startled me from sleep. Each is a hand
wearing authority's black leather glove;
they knock in counterpoint. What do they need?
Water, attention? Is this threat, command,
or inquiry? Or have these sentries scanned
the dawn horizon looking, not to feed,
but with a guardian's eye? One flies away;
the other pins me with one onyx bead
whose bailiff's glance says anything but love.
Well, sleep is over: he has brought the day.
And the day's thought: what is it he would say
that his companion failed to warn me of.

Ants

"Scurry" is not the word for what they do,
exactly, though we say so when we need
a word for ants in motion. See those two
tottering under crumbs "with all due speed,"

as legalese would term it, brick to brick
across the patio. Soundless (or maybe
we just don't hear them with an ear too thick
for such thin clamoring), they seem to see

us where we sit here snacking in the shade,
idling away the last September heat;
they move around our mass, but unafraid—
"due" seeming their one speed—between our feet

and out of range. Where is it they endure
their small transfigurations, form to form?
This is the way we know them, simple, sure,
unwelcome and predictable, the swarm

nevertheless amusing for an hour
spent without thoughts beside a garden pool,
observing that so much has ceased to flower
and how the afternoons are growing cool.

Enigma

Whether one shoot divided in mid-growth,
halved intimately lengthwise, face to face,
or, sprung from common soil that nurtured both,
two seedlings twined in their not-quite-embrace,
this maple—or these maples, who can say?—
cleave to what may be fiction—the one bole
rising "to heavenward"—and yet display
at once the cloven parts, the living whole.
Not that birds care which of the two it was—
fusion, divergence—reared their leafy town,
nor does its shade at noon cool less because
nobody knows. And when the leaves come down
they come down all together in one heap,
unmindful of what company they keep.

No Compass Points

No compass points, no up or down!
A chaos liberates the town—
and river too, that used to flow
through marshes where the herons go:
marsh, heron, town and river lost in snow.

Lovely, as if some spendthrift cloud
had torn and flung itself, a shroud
of manic silver drunk with light,
a plenitude so starkly bright
its wild perfection has the look of night.

So by degrees the ravished eye
begins to tire of stars that fly,
and yearns for fences, posts and trees—
faint frothy smears it almost sees—
like lovers' flaws and childhood fantasies.

What is our business, after all,
with such perfections as may fall
from heaven, or from any source?
The stuff we're made of sets our course
through each familiar jubilant remorse.

And why should we fear anything?
The year is our old rusty ring;
all chaos ends; the sky knows how,
and Earth is tilting even now,
measuring how much wildness to allow.

Stumbling

Since trees do half their growing out of sight,
with the blind tips of root hairs, underground,
my stumbling should not shock me so—by night,
an unfamiliar street—over a mound
coiling like serpents upward through a crack
in old cement: roots like a clot of veins,
a brooding varicosity, the black
tail of some hell-born dragon Beowulf's Danes
would have sent home. But here, there's neither axe
nor appetite for battle, no great harm,
only a little blood. These mock attacks
should not arouse the heart to such alarm—
did they not summon monsters poised to spring
out of the half-perceived in everything.

Suncatcher

Catch the sun just right in a small moon's
mirror you tilt a certain angle,
and you can spawn parabolas—a bangle
of spinning rays, haloes, balloons
elliptical with motion—flexing, sliding
up walls and down. Corners will make them crook
and bend; they send light under beds to look
for pennies dull with dust. What else is hiding,
since all housekeeping fails to some degree,
and every house harbors a niche inclined
to secrecy? Think how you, too, move blind
through rooms you think you know, if you're like me.
Until some idle game leads you to see
Small change you never thought—or meant—to find.

As If Some Jaded Reader

As if some jaded reader browsed the air,
riffled the pages of our summer trees,
and finding nothing worth perusing there
tossed every folio aside, the breeze
dismisses lightly what the light translates
from soil and water into each green tongue
the maple speaks. Its passing agitates
the leaves, but leaves them in their softly sung
monotony, impatient with the way
they, too, repeat themselves, like earthly hours.
This wind turns and returns, worries the day,
exhorting it to harness greater powers,
contrive a darker plot, matter less thin,
confront some story eager to begin.

Just Stopping

Exegesis

for Wesli Court

A droll poet—one Double-u Court—
Thinks ribbing the Lord is great sport.
I admire his pluck,
But I wish him good luck,
Since the Deity's temper is short.

In the Good Book, we see grim old Yahweh
Leaves no doubt that "It has to be MAH way!"
Not like Zeus and his pack,
Who are much more laid back
And run things in a loose, lah-dee-dah way.

To exclusive belief I say "Aw, no,"
Because why pick just one god? I dunno.
If one's good, why not more?
Say, twelve gods? Or a score?
I think poly is more fun than mono.

Gods were born out of thought metaphoric.
But people who wax dinosauric
Over figures of speech
Think they're factual, and preach
Their own myths as a dogma sophomoric.

Since we're courting Hellfire with this blather,
Let's go whole hog: admit that a Father
Who goes huffy and mute
Over one lousy fruit
Seems much less of a boon than a bother.

The thing that's most dear to my heart
Is not doctrines that tear us apart,
But each image or letter—
The more "graven" the better!—
That unites and enlightens through art.

Like those legends in which some Immortal
Lifts a maid past Divinity's portal
And engenders a hero!
As fact, that's a zero:
But a truth, if you read it as Court'll.

The Gods

"I've nothing else—to bring, You know—
So I keep bringing These—"

Emily Dickinson, #224

Nothing you promise satisfies them long.
What promises they make they seldom keep.
What earns their starkest wrath seems hardly wrong.
The darkest wrong takes place while they're asleep.

The love they're said to bear you is divine,
inscrutable, and nothing like your own.
Their only flesh is fire, is bread and wine,
is brooding stars and signs incised in stone.

They're not like saints: saints bleed, are born to feel
hunger, the lash of need and hope denied
before death strips them new: these are the real
thing, formless and unborn, and they abide.

What can you pledge to anchor them for good
to what you know, or make them speak to you?
Assent, belief, obedience? Nothing could.
Nothing you bring will coax them to be true.

Good News!

The known odds of something—or someone—living far,
far beyond the Earth increased dramatically on Monday.
New York Times, *November 5, 2013*

Good news! you think. Although, why should you care
what other life, light years away, may do
or be? Whether it is or isn't there—

wherever *there* is, in that lightless, bare
space our devices point and beckon to—
nothing will change for you. No one you care

about exists—or can—outside this air,
this cloudy bubble of desire, blue
oasis of habit. Seen out there,

even the sky you've always known must wear
a stranger's look, its undeciphered hue
a puzzle to the eye. And still, you care,

and think *Good news!* again, as if a stair
reached out across the void as sunbeams do,
inviting you to venture out, search there

for the imagined other—if you dare—
the hoped-for, fearful life that is not you,
that may not sense your presence, may not care.
If you can find it. If it's even there.

I Am the Hope

I am the hope that brought you to this day,
the flightless "thing with feathers" that just may
tell you the truth, for once, although by now
you've guessed I'd rather not, or don't know how.
But I know you—your wry, obsessive games—
and you know me, behind my scrim of names,
my eagerness to please, my lack of spine:
the arms that can't quite shield you, those are mine,
and mine the word you trust, lie after lie.
I am the last to turn and say goodbye.

If I Believed

If I believed in you, how could I trust
my treasured few, myself, to one like you,
so far, so hard to fathom, so unjust?
Yet if I did not want it to be true
that you are real and even know my face,
why would I tease this difficult belief
in distant love out of its hiding place?
A truce between us, then, to save us grief:
Let me not need you, whom I cannot know—
nor say I do, for fear—but turn instead,
for no cause but "because," to these below,
with whom I've traded shouts and songs and bread.
Forget me these last years, these two or ten,
until I near your house; surprise me then.

The Incorruptible

What is he doing
with all that lumber? she wonders;
where does he go
to be alone with
his unbearable god?

His lips are tight with
purpose; his eyes are glazed and flat;
he staggers in
and out with burdens
he will not talk about.

She likes him less than
ever: he will not join the dance,
drink beer, sit down
to toss a few dice
or gossip with neighbors.

Even their three sons,
reared in the desert of his ways,
are stiff as rods.
How glad she is for
the banter of their wives,

the stories traded
by old women at the fountain,
shrieks of children
wrangling at their games,
men shouting and singing.

From Noah she hears
only the tat-tat-tat of his
hammer as he
lays the keel of that
strange enormous coffin.

Just Stopping

The god in whom I once believed
showed up last night beside my bed,
and sat down at the foot. I said,
"What a surprise! Lord, I'm relieved
that you're not dead!"

He shrugged. "I have good days and bad.
When I was Zeus, what clout I had!
These days, it's all about complaints.
What thanks we get—it makes me mad—
goes to the saints

for curing stuff and granting things,
as if Creation were a mall
where every merchant has his stall.
And arguments: *You're made of strings,*
you're a big ball

of motion, you're a state of mind,
you're mathematics... on and on."
Now I could see his face was lined
like that of some old Mafia don
whose turf is gone.

And he looked tired, which, truth to tell,
He'd have to be by now, and bored,
unlike his counterpart in Hell,
and only fitfully adored.
He wasn't well.

I told him, "Look, you need some sleep;
lie down; I'll wake you when it's day,
and make you breakfast, if you stay."
But mumbling "...promises to keep...,"
he paled away.

When light returned, I knew I'd done
less than I should. But then, he'd run
too soon to hear what or how much
I might have said: *Thanks for the sun,*
or *Stay in touch.*

Lord of the Dance

This is Lord Shiva—gift of a young friend—
resting, in lotus posture, on my desk,
wearing three serpents and a rope, each hand
easy upon some weapon. Though his task
is dancing the universe to death and back
endlessly—for the joy of it!—he, too,
needs respite sometimes, and he takes this break
among unfinished poems and bills due.
They say he combs the Ganges from his head
down through his hair into its earthly grooves;
they say he'll whirl on graves to raise the dead,
uprooting what he sows; they chant his names—
"Destroyer," "The Auspicious," "He who moves
with equal grace to carnage and to games."

Lucifer Reminisces

A little action
is all we wanted at first
And you wonder why

The pool hall shut down
The bars all serving root beer
Rosie's boarded up

Glee club all day long
belting just *Glory, Glory*
It gets on your nerves

Now in these stinking
fumes it's not all peaches   But
you get used to things

The Man He Never Was but Meant to Be

The man he never was but meant to be
parted the curtains and approached the bed.
The doppelganger slept, blind to the red
blinking of unperturbed machinery.

The guest appraised him—that reality
he had been harnessed to, who was not dead—
and trembled—was it eagerness or dread?—
over the parting that would set him free.

The sleeper stirred and sighed, brought close to waking,
not by the click and hum of dials, but day,
tentative through the shades, carefully breaking.

Who was it sensed the other steal away—
a loss that seemed both blessing and forsaking?
Who was it said "Ego absolvo te"?

Marigolds

I know these gaudy ruffles as *clavel*
de muerto: "carnation of the dead,"
though nothing's grim about them but the smell.
They're not carnations, either: those are red
and white, mostly, like the barber pole's
reminder of bandages and gore,
or bullring tributes. These are tiny bowls
heaped with concentric yellows, from tight core
to ragged rim—old leather, butter, gold,
saffron and lemon, flax, pumpkin, maroon—
a lifetime's worth of autumns. "Of the old"
would be more apt than "of the dead," though soon
enough one is the other. May it be
easy, as trimming these I twist off some—
bent on their stems, or dull—and set them free
with one quick pinch of forefinger and thumb.

Post-Holiday

I've been thinking of you these wintry days,
now that your recent birthday once again
has spread its rumors of good will to men,
good news, good times, and songs of joyful praise.

The festive shops are jammed—now with returns,
rather than purchases—and trees are not
yet piled beside the curb, as is their lot
once they're denuded of their lights. Ours burns

with ornaments, and one still-unclaimed box
waits under it, in the belated glow
of glass and tinsel. But I hardly know
what links the man who'll wear those Argyle socks

to you, newborn in Nazareth, where kings
gave you much finer gifts, but could not save
you from a hard road to an early grave.
The season's full of bright, discordant things

that struggle with each other: hopeful singing,
gatherings of well-wishers eating well,
and Santa from the shelter with his bell,
clamoring for donations (hence the ringing)

intended for the hungry, strangers who
are out of work, or sick—again, or still—
or earn so little that one more debt will
likely put them out of doors, like you,

cold in the neighbor's crèche where you still lie.
Yes, you've been on my mind. But every baby
reminds me of my little boys, and maybe
works like those dreams in which an infant's cry

still sends me scrambling, troubled out of sleep.
Then I feel silly, awake, because my sons
are grown now. But the conscience stirs and runs
toward any human cry, as though to keep

an old promise whose force is never lost.
If I were given to belief, to prayer,
what would I pray for, and to whom? The air
is dry and sharp, and they're predicting frost.

Three Missives

I

Soldiers, or holy men you never knew,
scholars, or fishermen you moved among:
Yeshua ben Yusef, who can speak for you,
who spoke for all of us, and died so young?

II

Michael, Archangel, while the grownups prayed
I saw you trample Satan, raise your sword
too near the altar, over which the Lord
hung meek and bleeding. And I was afraid.

III

Think, Saul, how fearlessly we would today
construe the voice that struck you dumb and blind
with guilty zeal, if you had looked to find
Damascus by some common, bloodless way.

Torticollis

A *stiff-necked people:* that's your angry line.
And so we are, it's true, but not by choice,
but by your kingly planning and design,
so why the condemnation in your voice?

There's no denying, Lord, the bungle's yours:
you made these nerves too tense, sinews too tight,
these legs too long for crawling on all fours,
the spine too frail for facing you upright.

Father, make up your many-splendored mind,
as unlike ours as drought differs from rain:
either we are your *kinder*–so be kind!—
or failed experiments condemned to pain.
And will you hear me, see me, even if
I bend the neck you fashioned to be stiff.

The Unbeliever's Rosary

for Tim Murphy

Well, friend, you've done it now: and not with prayer
or argument to cure my unbelief,
or images of Hell, or of some stair
to heaven—but your illness, and my grief.
You clever fisherman of souls, the hook
you bait with that most powerful of lures—
stronger than any law in stone or book—
has snared me with one motive that ensures
final compliance: fear for those we love!
Look how, after so many years, these beads
wind through my fingers and remind me of
words meant to heal you; how each *Ave* leads,
almost, to childhood's wish: *Let this be true.*
You've done what hosts of angels could not do.

When Adam in the Grove Lay Sleeping

I

When Adam in the grove lay sleeping,
done with his labor,
a longing drove him near to weeping
for a soft neighbor

to lie beside him, on the green
and fragrant meadow,
enfold him close with nought between,
and cast one shadow.

Then Adam woke: Eve lay beside him
in virgin splendor,
in petal skin that mystified him,
and shawled with tender

ringlets like vines, whose dark profusion
suggested graces
that tempted him to slow intrusion
in hidden places.

When Heaven soured their costly fruit,
the angels wondered
why that strange couple, sadly mute,
would not be sundered.

But exiled Adam knew that Eve,
not Heaven's pardon,
was all there was he could not leave,

his only garden.

II

Eve, in her guardian's first embrace,
woke where he found her:
his touch, his scent, his voice and face
both pleased and bound her.

The crops he did not need to sow,
the plot he tended,
enclosed all she would need to know:
there, her world ended.

The serpent—living chain and jewel—
looped from the bough:
what pact, both generous and cruel,
would be sealed now?

"What have you done?" the gardener moaned,
"Now we are driven
into the wilderness, disowned
and unforgiven!"

As Adam stumbled, humble-hearted,
heavy with sin,
Eve's foot was light; the darkness parted
to let her in.

"So much to touch and taste!" she smiled,
"to learn, to be!"
And risk by risk she moved, beguiled,
and fallen free.

Overheard on Mount Sinai

But what if he's not *lovable?* As not
all neighbors are, of course: some beat their wives
and children, others talk nothing but rot
and do nothing worth doing all their lives.

I'm for commandments, yes, but love is no
hired menial summoned with *Come here!*
any more than the sun, or wind, or snow.
Obedience will come running; so will fear;

but will they stay the night? The watchman leaves,
and they slip out unseen. Sometimes, it's true,
we can be just; and when a neighbor grieves,
we can be kindly. But can even you
demand *love...as thyself...* from flesh and bone?
Everything's easy to inscribe in stone.

All Points

When God was apprehended at the border
he meant to cross to vanish from our sight,
they brought him, handcuffed, to some law-and-order
prosecutorial type who spent the night
questioning him: old crimes, and where had he
been at the hour of this and that. He said
nothing. The young defender hastily
summoned by phone, who had been roused from bed
and had not even shaved, observed his client
for any help—exculpatory claim,
hint of an alibi—from this defiant
regal thug who would not give his name,
the charges brought against him likely true,
and little left, within the law, to do.

Upon Encountering a New Image of an Old Friend

*"With God at Our Desks: The Rise of Religion and Evangelism in the
American Workplace"*   *—Russell Shorto*

I found your picture in the Sunday *Times*
between two men—no, not accused of crimes
and crucified with you, but shaking hands.
One basks in your broad smile; the other stands,
alert, waiting his turn, right palm turned up
like a come-hither or a beggar's cup.

Times Magazine, October thirty-one,
two-oh-oh-four, cover: something well done
clearly concluded, the good deal is closed,
the briefcase-carrier leaving, both men posed,
eager, in suit and tie, wearing the white
shirt of middle management. The light
from some downtown's lit windows gilds your hair,
your well-cut beard, the robe draped with much care
over one shoulder.

                  I remember other
pictures of you, before which my grandmother
kept candles burning—each in its clean dish—
not to beseech the granting of some wish
(as here, paragraph two, for "the best buyer..."
or "money to purchase...") but out of desire
beyond desire. In one, your mother's veil
covered you while you slept; in one, your pale
and ravaged form was washed and laid to rest;

another had you pointing at your breast,
sadly, as if inviting us to gaze
into the thorn-crowned heart, pierced and ablaze.

But in this photo-op from the Midwest,
you're clearly prospering, and doing best
among the very merchants you turned out,
once, from the temple, with an angry shout.

How shall old love regard what becomes strange,
though love—or so says Paul—endures all change?
How to discern false images from true?
It's crossed my mind that none of these is you.

Naked

...and Dangerous

I had a bad pain...and in spite of it I couldn't wait
to start writing. You know how it is when the muse
assaults you...   —Yala Korwin

WANTED for assault: known as "The Muse,"
ARMED (with a deadly lyre). She stalks her prey
and tends to strike by night; is known to use
impersonation to secure her way
into the victim's dreams and waking hours;
locks have proved ineffectual, as have seals
upon the heart and memory. No powers
of conscious mind deter her, no appeals
to mercy or to duty. Do not seek
to overwhelm her by brute will or guile!
Surrender what she asks of you, and speak
only with her leave, and only while
under the full force of her attack.
Obey her, and—who knows?—she may come back.

Browsing

Down aisles of crowded shelves and up again
I revel, rich with this whole afternoon
squandered on browsing. Old friends well met
greet me from the stained windows of their verse,

sing, ruminate, beguile me with stanzas
intimate as wine. Here's one remembers
his Julia gowned in silk; one mourns her God;
another, in turning weather, his thirtieth year.

And down this way, sleeker, in paperback,
new names stroke me like hands, whisper Listen
from lamplit border towns, from steaming cities,
wheatfields, the sodden moors. They are lucid,

they anchor each thing to its absence
like a tree to its shadow; yet their music
calls me by name, pays back what it costs, heals,
redeems each loss by naming it.

Their voices lift me, in one long communion
feed me their grace, as if a heart could open
itself like a ripe melon on the plate
of these pages, saying "Eat, this is for you."

Dare

You need to try a triolet?
Go on, but you'll be hooked. For good
or ill, it's what you can't forget
you need to try. A triolet
is one last drink, is that sure bet,
is nagging lust. You want—you should—
you need—to try a triolet:
go on. But you'll be hooked for good.

Degas

I don't like your green women, your mauve
women who lower their haunches into tubs,
turning their heads. Your dancers keep their distance,
even rubbing dirty feet on half-lit stages
or stretching between their numbers; your fallen rider
is self-contained on his flat green field, he
does not look at us, he is past all looking.
But your green women turn their toweled heads
to find us; the blue hollows of their eyes
want to tell us something they've learned. Your ironers
yawn over the world's damp laundry: we know
what they know, the streets beyond that window,
the repetition of gold and blue mornings,
stiffness between the shoulders; but what
can we make of your green women, your mauve
women who lower iridescent flesh
into their tubs, into those shallow graves?

Dry Spell

The soil in this old pot, dry for too long,
in which no trace of growth seemed worth the tending,
amazes me this morning by unbending
one pale green arch—as if to prove me wrong—
into a slender spine tensing erect,
tossing its cowl of dust, riding the air.
So much for the surmise that nothing's there;
something thrives, in silence, on neglect.

I had forgotten how concrete sprouts leaves;
forgotten how the living resurrect
the gestures of the dead; how on a bare
brown limb, tangled and ugly where it clings
pulsing in its dark web, the larva weaves
a mottled incongruity of wings.

Escher

First, as a skein of geese migrating these
few inches left to right, they stir the cloud
they beat their way through by minute degrees
into a restless grid, a craze, a crowd,
a froth of dots like those that swarm behind
closed lids or bubble in a petri dish.
Then some—somehow, but how? but yes—will find
their skein transformed into a school of fish.
Lovely, this fable, how the skin breaks down
between the flyer and the swimmer, how
air and water, the unyielding brown
hide of the Earth itself, parts to allow
this fusion of unlikes, as if conspiring
to grant the final wish of all desiring.

The Inventor of the Metaphor

"La noche está negra como la boca de un lobo."
                              —Spanish saying
"The night is black as the mouth of a wolf."

Render me slight and vigilant, with more
cunning than strength, and now less swift
in my old age—I'm thirty—than before.
Grant me a sharpened stick. Around me, lift
a scrim of forest, and above me, stars
I've learned to follow when the light is gone
and I'm far from the fire. Dress me in scars
not visible this long before the dawn,
but touchable, and let the darkness be
alive with snouts. And now I dare to think—
invent—this monstrous thought: *All I can see
is wolf: stars in the stream are eyes that blink;
the wind, wolf's breath; the briar's thorn, his claw;
the night open to take me, the wolf's maw.*

Metrics

I like the clattering of hoof on street
signaling *horse*: slow course of fruit
from earth, air, water, sun and root
through branch to ripened flower makes it sweet;

under soul's music, the eternal tone,
I like mortality to play the bass;
love and the dancer's gestures must be grace
wrested from bone.

All things, however magneted by cause,
should bear their nature's imprint to the end:
should shadow forth the whole to which they tend,
but keep small laws.

Neither Snow, nor Rain...

Hermes in winged sandals was not more
feared or longed-for than this mild young man
in sturdy shoes trudging toward our front door,
bearing the daily mail. Amiable, tan
as his Olympian avatar, soft-spoken
and fond of banter, he may hazard, say,
some wry and feigned complaint, his stride unbroken,
or quip about the weather; then away
to bless the neighbors. For my smile and nod,
he trades a bundle in a rubber band.

Now I examine what this casual god
has brought today, light in his neutral hand:
one more polite rejection there, and here
a birth announcement; what more doctors find
in a friend's X-ray; what desire and fear
spelled on the nightly keyboard of the mind,
refuted or confirmed.

               If he could change
his freight at will, would he bear golden luck
for just a chosen few? Would he arrange
nothing but joy served from his small white truck?
Would it be better to believe he knows
the doom he bears, and yearns to hold it back?
All foolish fantasy. And there he goes,
our charioteer, rounding the cul-de-sac
and braking house to house.

               There are new breeds

of messenger whose dry communication
plies swift and clear; across the screen it leads
each moment's bolts of anguish and elation
to flicker from afar in a small sky.
Better this ancient route, this human face,
this comrade's touch, Fate deigning to put by
divinity, and stooping to our place.

O, Paradiso

Old platters that we sang to long ago—
seventy-eights in faded sleeves—are stacked
awaiting resurrection through the slow
transfer onto CDs. Though warped and cracked,
though scratchy, they evoke—even unheard—
decades inscribed in vinyl as in rhyme.
In one, the Andrew Sisters give their word
to be with us in apple blossom time;
here, Nat King Cole spills his brown silky grief,
that stardust memory of love gone by;
here, in the light of flares, the soldier's sheaf
of mail from the home front; and here, the cry
Caruso turns to song, long stilled by then:
"O, Paradiso" will not come again.

The Poet Attempts a Firm Resolve During a Long Dry Spell

I've made my mind up, and I'll say it once:
Muse, you've had all of me you're going to get.
What else did you expect, after these months
of silence and neglect? I pine, and let
the suitors feast without me, lone, alert
for the least whispered sign of your return,
and where are you? Spoiled lover, heartless flirt,
I trace your far philandering while I burn
tormented by cruel rumors: here a prize
I hankered for gone to some witless hack,
and there another published—damn her eyes—
by that prestigious journal I can't crack.
Relent, you say? Never! But what's the use?
I know your wiles, how soon your gifts begin
to trickle in: the dozen clever, loose
rhymes, fresh-picked, come-hithering like sin,
that single long-stemmed metaphor I pluck
just before sleep descends. That's how it goes:
you're back, I sigh, you have your way, my luck!
And how this long affair will end, god knows.

A Reader Congratulates Me on Being Both Quotable and Still Alive

He writes that he's my junior by one year:
I think I can guess why
he's both surprised and glad that I'm still here.
Well, so am I.

And glad, too, that one aging, kindly man—
the boy that he once was—
recalls a poem he says I wrote, and can
quote it—and does,

from memory—apologizing for
just one misquoted line.
Moving, yes: would it move me even more
if it *were* mine?

I don't know whose it is, or where he found it,
or why he remains sure
it's mine, or what his memory weaves around it:
errors endure.

Would it be wrong to thank him (and keep mum)
for praise I didn't earn?
Truth is an iffy thing, often, for some,
too late to learn.

But never mind: the author—he or she—
will surely be forgiving
with old, unwilling plagiarists like me
still busy living.

Still Another Ars Poetica

To sing it better, let the words say less
but sing more, farther than their sense can go:
dole them out with your fingers, stress by stress.

Some say you need to shout it, to confess
truth like a fever on the lip, but no,
I say to sing it truer, say it less.

A flame is cooled and quenched by quick excess,
but burns like diamonds if it's embered low;
bank it down with your fingers, stress by stress.

Oblique is how it's done: divert, digress,
point where it isn't, look away just so.
They'll hear you better if you tell them less,

Or tell it bit by bit, under duress,
as if some chain that bound you head to toe
left only fingers free to speak distress.

Hint, as a gossip hints to make them guess;
make it a game of hide-and-almost-show
with wizard fingers, not to feel it less
but better, truer, longer for the stress.

Work in Progress

He showed me some, and asked for my advice.
I pointed out a line that wouldn't scan,
a pair of rhymes that cried for a divorce,
and commented—but briefly—on the quotes
in foreign alphabets, unglossed. "Of course,"
he said, and nodded, and took notes,
as if OK with all of it.

               And then
I added, "Put back every *the* and *an*
and *a*. It's almost nothing, what they do,
but articles make what they say ring true."

You never know what buttons not to touch,
which *almost nothing*'s going to prove too much.
This morning he submitted work again,
but brusque, defensive, with a hint of spice.
Only fool goes for walk in minefield twice:
next time I'll tell him poem is very nice.

Naked

"Naked," my father said, waving a hand
that swept aside the audience in the hall.
"Picture them wearing nothing but their skin,
nothing at all."

The auditorium where I soon would read—
for the first time!—now filled with men of letters
whose poems filled fat books. And I sixteen,
and they my betters.

Papa had made me laugh away my fear—
what silly images he'd made me see!—
and so I read, and they, in their undress,
applauded me.

The nakedness of audiences remains
my father's spell, effective to this day.
I would undress upon the page. But that,
he didn't say.

Revision

The woman I judged hastily (she wore
bizarre, revealing clothes and flashy boots)
stood up to read, but I heard nothing more
after two lines assailed my absolutes
with how she lived her life, with what she seemed.
Just yesterday I found a most austere,
most tender poem of hers. Last night I dreamed
she came to visit me. My mother's fear,
my mother's mother's judgments, primly clothed
in the whalebone assumptions of their youth,
exhorted me to loathe *what must be loathed.*
But in my dream, her silence stirred a truth
that wrestled with their gloss upon the good,
And what she left unsaid, I understood.

Wind-Chimes

It means to be an instrument, this thing
dangling where no wind stirs, without a sound:
one small pagoda roof and five brass rods
and four Chinese medallions, on clear string.
Blow on it lightly and it spins around,
dust swirling slowly. The pagoda nods,
as if it had all day to come unwound
and wound again, before it speaks for gods
who take their time with what they have to say,
inscribed on these medallions: some profound
prophecy, surely! Or maybe "ting-a-ling."
Hang it where it may fall—in the wind's way—
or rust, or shatter. It was meant to play.
It needs some fiercer breath to make it sing.

For the Poets

In Frost Country

When I see birches
dipping to earth from heaven
you're riding in them
And then you step down
from the crown   What care you take
that no branch will break

Upstairs in Amherst

The whiteness of it
cries out   The curve of each sleeve
aches unceasingly
and every button
from neck to hemline   Alive
Burns in its prison

Yawp

What road on this earth
is not blessed by the bootsoles
of your unbounded
song   Or the hunger
of your time-traveling eyes
Walt   Tender father

Made in the USA
Middletown, DE
11 July 2019